Aberdeenshire Library and Information Service
www.aberdeenshire.gov.uk/libraries
Renewals Hotline 01224 661511

TOWNSEND, John

Outrageous
inventions

A Weird History of Science

Outrageous Inventions

John Townsend

www.raintreepublishers.co.uk

Visit our website to find out more information about **Raintree** books.

To order:
☎ Phone 44 (0) 1865 888112
▤ Send a fax to 44 (0) 1865 314091
▢ Visit the Raintree bookshop at **www.raintreepublishers.co.uk** to browse our catalogue and order online.

MONKEY PUZZLE MEDIA LTD
Produced for Raintree by
Monkey Puzzle Media Ltd
Gissing's Farm, Fressingfield
Suffolk IP21 5SH, UK

First published in Great Britain by Raintree,
Halley Court, Jordan Hill, Oxford OX2 8EJ,
part of Harcourt Education.
Raintree is a registered trademark
of Harcourt Education Ltd.

Editor: Steve Parker
Designer: Tim Mayer
Picture Researcher: Lynda Lines
Production: Chloe Bloom

Originated by Modern Age
Printed and bound in China
by South China Printing Company

10 digit ISBN 1 4062 0559 1
13 digit ISBN 978 1 4062 0559 6
11 10 09 08 07
10 9 8 7 6 5 4 3 2 1

British Library Cataloguing in Publication Data
Townsend, John, 1955–
Outrageous inventions. – (A weird history of science)
1.Inventions – History – Juvenile literature
2.Technological innovations – History – Juvenile literature
I.Title
609

Acknowledgements
Advertising Archives p. **38**; AKG-Images p. **22** (British Library); Alamy Images p. **40** (brt PHOTO); Brown and Michaels PC p. **29**; Colitz/Edward P. Dutkiewicz p. **42**; Concord Confections p. **5 bottom right**, **35 bottom**; Katherine Dunn p. **23**; Corbis pp. **5 middle right** (China Photos), **9 top right**, **12** (Austrian Archives), **17** (Hulton-Deutsch Collection), **19** (Angelo Cavalli/Zefa), **24**, **25** (Elberto Estevez/EPA), **26** (Bettmann), **27** (Hulton-Deutsch Collection), **28** (Bettmann), **30** (Hulton-Deutsch Collection), **31** (Bettmann), **32** (Bettmann), **36** (China Photos), **37** (Annie Griffiths Belt), **45** (Rick Friedman), **47** (Neville Elder); Getty Images pp. **5 top right**, **6**, **7**, **8**, **10**, **13**, **15**, **16**, **18**, **21**, **44**; Mary Evans Picture Library pp. **11**, **20**, **33**, **43**; Moller International p. **1**, **14**; Science Photo Library pp. **4** (Christian Jegou/Publiphoto Diffusion), **35 top** (Du Cane Medical Imaging Ltd), **39** (Andrew Syred), **48** (Roger Harris), **49** (Victor Habbick Visions); Topfoto.co.uk pp. **5 top left**, **9 bottom left** (National Motor Museum/HIP), **41**, **46** (Empics).

Cover photograph of a hand-held radio transmitter and receiver reproduced with permission of Black Star/Alamy.

Every effort has been made to contact copyright holders of any material reproduced in this book. Any omissions will be rectified in subsequent printings if notice is given to the publishers.

Contents

Any words appearing in the text in bold,
like this, are explained in the glossary.
You can also look out for them in the "Word
bank" at the bottom of each page.

Bright ideas

Before there were patents, anyone could steal an inventor's ideas. A lifetime's work could be copied by someone else, then made and sold. This is why many scientists kept their experiments secret. Then other people couldn't steal the results and claim them as their own.

What is the greatest invention of all time? You might choose the computer, the television, or the mobile phone. But what about the aeroplane, the petrol (gasoline) engine, or various kinds of plastics? Maybe you would choose more everyday things like light bulbs, flush toilets, or even chips.

Long ago, great inventions such as the plough and the wheel changed forever what people could do. For thousands of years since, great minds and hard work have come up with machines, gadgets, devices, and all kinds of amazing inventions – so that today we cannot imagine life without them.

Leonardo da Vinci (1452–1519) not only painted famous works of art such as the *Mona Lisa*. He also kept notebooks of scientific designs and inventions, although only a few were actually made.

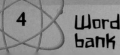
patent special document giving only the inventor the right to make and sell the invention

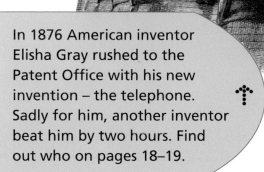

In 1876 American inventor Elisha Gray rushed to the Patent Office with his new invention – the telephone. Sadly for him, another inventor beat him by two hours. Find out who on pages 18–19.

Becoming an inventor

It's amazing how people invented so much, so long ago, with so few tools and materials. Even when machines and gadgets were finally finished, they were often thought by others to be worthless, dangerous or totally outrageous. Some inventors even had their great ideas stolen.

Today, to make sure no one steals your idea or copies your invention, you need to **patent** it. A patent examiner decides if the idea really is new. Then your invention is given a number, which gives only you the right to make or sell your idea. Hey presto, you've joined the millions of inventors who have changed the world!

Find out later

Who thinks that one day we will all have personal flying machines?

How did a pesky plant lead to a super-sticky invention?

Who chewed over a sticky problem and came up with a bubbly idea?

Risky travel

As soon as the wheel was invented, people could think about "travel machines". At first these were just chariots pulled by horses or ox-drawn carts. Then inventors found ways to replace animals with engines.

The first mechanical road vehicle was a steam-powered army tractor invented by Nicolas-Joseph Cugnot (1725–1804) of France. It moved at just 4 kilometres per hour (2.5 miles per hour), slower than the average walking speed. It had to stop every 10 minutes to build up steam. In 1771 Cugnot crashed it into a wall, and became the first person to have a motor accident!

Did you know?

Before people began to travel by train, some scientists thought our bodies would not survive going at high speeds. In about 1835 Professor Dionysius Lardner said: "Rail travel at high speed is not possible because passengers, unable to breathe, would die."

George Stephenson's *Rocket*, built in 1829, was not the first steam locomotive. However its new design made it faster and this design has been used by nearly all steam engines since.

Word bank   fad short-lived fashion or interest

Paul Daimler takes his father Gottlieb for a drive in the first four-wheeled Daimler car, 1886.

Fears

It took many more years before petrol motor cars arrived. In 1885 German inventor Karl Benz built the world's first car powered by an **internal combustion** (petrol-type) engine. The same year Gottlieb Daimler developed a petrol-engined vehicle. Even before these cars first appeared, many people were worried by the invention of gasoline (petrol) as a fuel:

"The dangers are obvious. Horseless carriages propelled by gasoline might attain speeds of even 20 miles per hour (32 kilometres per hour). The menace to people of vehicles of this type hurtling through our streets and poisoning the atmosphere ... would be overwhelming."

Some of the fears in this 1875 United States Congressional Record – such as **pollution** and speed – were absolutely right.

Here to stay

Henry Ford (1863–1947) began mass-producing cars in the early 20th century. His bank manager warned. "The horse is here to stay, but the automobile is only a **fad**."

By 1914, Ford's Michigan factory took just 93 minutes to make a complete Model T car. Today there are more than 600 million motor vehicles in the world.

---

internal combustion when power comes from fuel burning in an enclosed space
pollution chemicals, particles or rubbish that spoil or damage nature

Burning rubber

Imagine a car without tyres. Your journey would be very bumpy and dangerous! A strange discovery led to a special type of rubber that made it possible to produce tyres.

The problem with ordinary rubber was that it went gooey in warm weather and brittle when cold. Charles Goodyear (1800–1860) dreamed of making all-weather rubber. In an experiment he mixed liquid rubber with chemicals, then painted the mix on to fabric. Nothing happened until he left the rubberized fabric on a hot stove by mistake. Goodyear looked at the sizzling, smelly rubber and was amazed. It hadn't melted into goo – it remained solid. Tyre rubber was born.

Did you know?

Charles Goodyear did not become rich from inventing his new type of rubber. He died very poor, owing a lot of money. The famous Goodyear Tyre and Rubber Company began in 1898, many years after his death. It used his name to honour his great invention.

Charles Goodyear shows how his new way of heating rubber makes it tough and non-sticky.

Word bank

pneumatic worked by air, such as pumping air under pressure

Rubber in court

In 1844 Goodyear managed to get a **patent** for his new rubber. He called it **"vulcanized"** after Vulcan, the Roman god of fire. Another scientist called Horace Day began making the same tough rubber to sell. Goodyear took him to court in New Jersey, United States, for stealing his invention.

The court had to decide which man first added chemicals to rubber and heated it to make it extra tough. Goodyear's lawyer gave a strong speech on how Goodyear alone had discovered the new rubber. "Is there a man in the world who found out that fact before Charles Goodyear?" The court believed him and Goodyear won his case.

Modern racing cars depend on wide tyres of tough, gripping rubber to stay on the track.

Air-filled tyres

In 1888 John Dunlop's son rode his tricycle, with solid rubber tyres, over bumpy cobbles. To make the ride smoother, Dunlop put thin rubber sheets around the wheels, glued them into tubes, and pumped them with air. He had invented the first **pneumatic** tyre. In 1889, Dunlop opened his first tyre factory in Dublin, Ireland.

After John Dunlop fitted wheels with "air cushion" hose pipe tyres, his son Johnny had a much smoother ride.

vulcanize   treat rubber with chemicals and heat to give it strength

Safety on the road

"Why didn't I think of that?" people ask themselves, as they use some of the most familiar and simple inventions.

At a time when all car-makers were men, a woman came up with one of the best-ever ideas for motor vehicles. In 1903 Mary Anderson was on a bus to New York. The driver had to keep getting out to wipe snow from the windscreen. Mary had an idea for a blade, operated by a lever inside the bus, to sweep the screen clear. It could be taken off in warm weather. Anderson received a **patent** for her windscreen wiper in 1905.

Safety reflectors

Without street lights or extra-powerful headlamps, how could night drivers see the road? Glass **reflectors** or "cat's eyes" now shine back at us. This simple idea was invented by Percy Shaw in 1933, after he drove along a winding road on a foggy night. He was saved from going in a ditch by a cat beside the road, whose eyes reflected his car's lights.

Percy Shaw (1890–1976) got a patent for his cat's eyes, began making them in his own factory and soon made his fortune.

jaywalker someone on a road who pays little attention to traffic
pedestrian walking person

The Jaywalker Scoop sucked careless pedestrians into a scoop and made them run on a treadmill. Of course it was never built!

Pedestrian trouble

When people began driving cars, one problem was how to warn **pedestrians** to get out of the way. People tried everything from motor horns to someone walking along in front of the car waving a flag.

Some car-makers came up with truly outrageous inventions. The 1921 Pedestrian Pusher had a wire grill on the front of the car, to scoop up pedestrians and tip them out of the way rather than knock them over. It was not a serious answer to the pedestrian problem!

Bizarre idea

Early motorists often had problems with people stepping out in front of them. Some of the magazines of the 1920s had cartoons of zany inventions to deal with **jaywalkers**. Gradually real inventions, like loud car horns and the stripes of the pedestrian crossing, helped with this problem.

reflector object which bounces back or reflects light

Up, up, and away

For centuries people dreamed of travelling long distances by flying like birds, using their arms and legs to power themselves.

In about 1490 Leonardo da Vinci studied the flight of birds and realized that humans are not strong enough to fly using arms and legs alone. That didn't stop him designing an **ornithopter**. This was an aircraft with wings that flapped, like a bird's wings. Later inventors tried different types of ornithopter. However none of them could keep a person in the air for more than a few seconds, let alone travel across the sky.

Flapping flying machines

There were many attempts through history to build the flying craft known as ornithopters or "flapping machines". Some were made before the name "ornithopter" was invented in 1799. Several designs were more like parachutes that could glide down from a hot-air balloon.

Clockmaker and inventor Jakob Degen, of Austria, designed this craft in 1807. It was a cross between a glider and double-parachute.

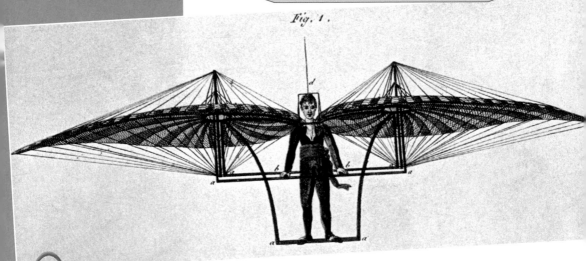

Fig. 1.

Word bank

ornithopter flying machine with wings that flap like a bird's

In July 1874, Vincent De Groof's craft failed and he fell to his death in front of a stunned crowd in London, England.

Scary aircraft

James Clark of Pennsylvania, USA made clocks, repaired bicycles and invented flying machines. He developed an aircraft during the early 1900s but it was wrecked. Clark rebuilt it with an engine in 1907. However, the Wright brothers had already made the first aircraft in 1903, so they beat him into the record books.

Deadly inventions

Louis Charles Letur invented a flying machine in the 1850s, with wings and a tail for steering. These failed when a gust of wind caught his machine just as he was gliding down from a balloon in London in 1854. Letur was killed when his invention smashed into some trees.

Not put off by this accident, ten years later a Belgian shoemaker and inventor called Vincent De Groof made a hang-glider with beating wings. His plan was to cut it loose from a balloon 350 metres (1,150 feet) above the ground and glide down in front of a cheering crowd. But the wings broke and De Groof dropped to his death.

Above the clouds

How would you like to take off from your own doorstep or driveway? One day cars might fly!

Since the 1960s Paul Moller of the United States has spent US$100 million developing his flying car. He believes that one day people will launch Skycars from their rooftops. "I know this technology is coming, and if I don't do it someone else will," Moller said. He built his first version, the M220X, in 1962. His current project is the M400, which looks like a small fighter plane. No one outside his company has seen the Skycar fly freely through the sky – yet!

Cars that fly

For over 100 years, people have tried making cars that fly. The United States Patent Office has about 80 **patents** for various kinds of flying car. Some, like the M200X, look more like flying saucers. Most have never taken off. Even those that can fly cannot travel long distances.

N7164J

MOLLER SKYCAR

Is it a bird, is it a plane ... no, it's a Skycar! "I think we will be out there with these vehicles by 2008," says the M400's inventor Paul Moller.

Word bank

solo done by or for one person

Personal "plane"

Michael Moshier is another American trying to invent a machine for **solo** flying. According to him, his Solotrek XFV has flown a few centimetres above the ground for about nine seconds. A metal frame supports two fans powered by small engines. The pilot stands on a pair of footrests, straps on a body belt and works two hand controllers.

The plan is for Solotrek to travel at more than 120 kilometres per hour (75 miles per hour) at heights of up to 2.5 kilometres (1.5 miles). It looks like something from a science fiction story – but it would be great for zooming into town!

Will it ever happen?

In 1943 aircraft expert Harry Bruno said: "Instead of a car in every garage, there will be a helicopter. These 'copters will be so safe and will cost so little to produce, that small models will be made for teenage youngsters. These tiny 'copters, when school lets out, will fill the sky – as the bicycles of our youth filled the roads."

Get ready for take-off! Michael Moshier models his Solotrek XFV. You could have your own personal helicopter soon – if you have up to £100,000 to spare!

15

Great gadgets at home

Many homes today are full of gadgets that we hardly think about until they go wrong. Most of them came about through sheer hard work, real struggle, and pure **genius**.

Let there be light

We rarely think twice about flicking on a light switch. Yet the electric light bulb took years of research. Early electric lights were tested in a few American streets in the 1870s but they quickly burned out. American inventor Thomas Edison tried thousands of different types of material for the filament (the wire inside that glows). In 1879, he discovered that a carbon wire in an oxygen-free bulb glowed for more than 1,500 hours.

Edison and his team test their new electric lamp in October 1879, in their Menlo Park laboratory.

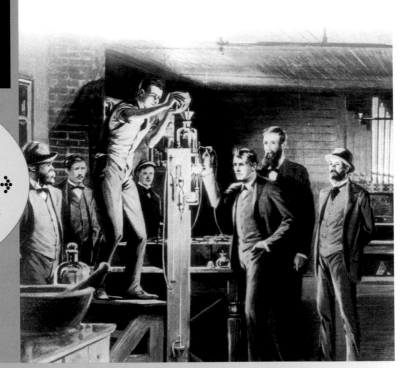

Word bank

genius very gifted person with great abilities
inspiration having a great thought or idea

Few inventors are as famous as Thomas Edison. Yet when he was young, his schoolteachers said he was dull and could not be taught! How wrong could they be? His mother taught him at home instead. She clearly had great success.

Thinking big

As Edison became successful he built the world's first scientific research centre, Menlo Park, in 1876. He and his staff often worked on more than 40 projects at a time, including the phonograph, the motion-picture camera, and the microphone. In 1887 Edison built a new centre, West Orange, which was ten times bigger. It is now a United States national historical park.

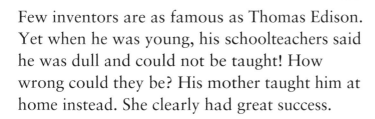

Years of hard work

Although people called Edison a genius, he said that "genius is one percent **inspiration** and 99 percent **perspiration**". In other words, inventing was hard work. Edison also said: "To invent you need a good imagination and a pile of junk." He often spent 100 hours a week in his workshops.

Thomas Edison first recorded sounds on wax-covered cylinders. Then came wind-up gramophones like these, playing flat discs. Today's MP3 players are far easier to carry!

perspiration sweat

17

"It's for you"

Sending voice messages over long distances was once thought to be impossible. That was until Alexander Graham Bell (1847–1922) invented something he called a telephone. In 1876 the first words to crackle along telephone wires were: "Come here, Watson, I want you." Bell was calling to his assistant in another room, after accidentally spilling some chemicals. Watson heard the call through the telephone that Bell had just designed.

Four years later Bell said: "One day there will be a telephone in every major city in the United States." He knew his invention was important, but he had no idea that in the future there would be millions of telephones in every city, and almost everywhere else too. Imagine what he would think of today's picture-taking, word-texting, TV-receiving mobile phones.

Alexander Bell (1847–1922) made the first long-distance telephone call from New York to Chicago in 1892.

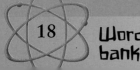
Word bank

telegraph method of sending messages along wires as code signals, such as Morse Code

A close call

As Alexander Bell worked on his invention, he did not know that nearby another inventor, Elisha Gray, was also inventing a telephone. Neither knew about the other. They both asked for a **patent** for their telephones at the New York Patent Office on the same day in 1876. Bell beat Gray by only two hours. In fact, Gray's telephone was still not quite finished. It was a very close call but finally Bell was given the patent.

Within a few years, the Bell Telephone Company had made Alexander a millionaire, and the telephone was an important everyday item around the world.

No value?

In 1876 the Western Union **Telegraph** Company decided: "The telephone has too many shortcomings to be seriously considered as a means of communication. The device is of no value." Yet a few years later, in 1883, the first telephone link between two cities connected New York and Boston. Today mobile phones are used across the whole United States.

The modern mobile phone or cellphone network covers most of the world, even the Himalayan mountains of Tibet.

Keeping clean

Housework has been a daily chore for people throughout the ages. Houses with coal fires and stoves used to get very sooty and dusty. Floors had to be swept and scrubbed often. Then someone came up with the great idea of a machine that could suck up all the dirt.

In 1901 Hubert Booth of London invented an electric vacuum cleaner. It was so large that its pump and motor had to be carried on a horse-drawn cart. A long hose pipe was unrolled into the house, with at least two people operating it. Some house-owners even invited friends round to enjoy the "vacuum party"!

Success at last

Between 1978 and 1993, James Dyson of England built 5,000 trial designs for a new vacuum cleaner. His efforts didn't impress the Hotpoint Company. In 1982 they turned down his new design. A Hotpoint boss said: "This project is dead from the neck up." Within 10 years Dyson was selling over a third of all vacuum cleaners in Britain.

In the early 1900s all you needed to clean inside your home was a vacuum cleaner like this, outside your home.

sensor device that detects what is nearby

The Roomba is an "intelligent floorvac". It can move around furniture and cope with floor surfaces such as carpets, wood, and tiles.

Did you know?

A company called iRobot began selling robot vacuum cleaners in 2002. The Roomba is a small, disc-shaped cleaner that cruises around a room, using **sensors** to get round furniture and avoid stairs. The design has been improved each year. By 2006 more than 1.5 million Roombas had been sold, making it the most successful home robot so far.

A century of sucking dirt

In 1905 the designers Chapman and Skinner of San Francisco invented a smaller, lighter electric vacuum cleaner. It still weighed more than 40 kilograms (88 pounds) and used a fan 45 centimetres (18 inches) across to produce the suction. Imagine the noise!

Next, inventor James Spangler worked on an even lighter electric suction cleaner in 1908. He sold the invention to his cousin's husband, William Hoover. They started the Hoover Electric Suction Sweeper Company. The famous "hoover" was born.

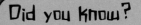

Just so you know

A vacuum is a space that has had all or most of the air removed from it, usually with a pump. The first vacuum pump was invented by German physicist Otto von Guericke in 1650.

Down the drain

Can you imagine life without the toilet? In England in 1596, John Harrington invented a flush toilet for Queen Elizabeth I. Most people had to wait many hundreds of years before ordinary homes had the luxury of their own plumbed-in toilet.

For centuries people just had "chamber pots" in their houses, which they often kept under their beds. These had to be emptied outside each day. Or people used a bucket or hole in the ground outside, whatever the weather. When scientists began to understand disease and **hygiene**, toilets that flushed away waste became important for healthy cities. Drains and sewers were built to carry away the waste.

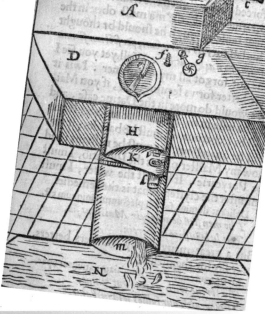

Writer John Harrington (1561–1612) designed the first flush toilet, which became known as the WC (water closet) or "privy".

Word bank

cistern tank for storing water

Making a splash

In 1857 the first American **patent** was given for a flushing toilet called the plunger closet. Many similar ideas followed. Between 1910 and 1930 about 350 different types of flushing toilet were invented in the United States alone.

Today's toilets come in many designs. Some flush automatically when the user stands up or moves away. One toilet **cistern** is a glass aquarium with fish in it. Fortunately, the fish aren't disturbed when it is flushed.

In 1998 the singing toilet lid was invented. "The average person spends over 2,500 hours on the toilet in 80 years," said Swiss inventor Roger Weisskopf. "I thought we needed more fun in there."

Can you believe it?

In the United States in 1980, a patent was given for a pet toilet! A ramp leads up to a box on top of a normal toilet. After the pet does its "daily duty", a sensing device opens a trap door. The waste falls into the toilet, which automatically flushes. Your pet no longer has to leave the house!

Toilets with extra features are now fashion items in many homes.

Homes of tomorrow

Technology develops so fast that new gadgets for the home are big business. In 1998 a Japanese company invented a refrigerator smart enough to keep track of what is inside, and order replacements on the Internet for home delivery.

Thirty years ago, no one imagined how computers would change so many homes. In 1977 Ken Olson, president of Digital Equipment Corporation (DEC), said: "There is no reason anyone would want a computer in their home." How wrong he was! Who knows how computers will change home life in the next 20 or 30 years?

Early robots

- George Moore of the United States made a walking machine in the 1890s. A steam engine drove its legs. This "Steam Man" walked in circles around a post.
- In 1939 a human-like walking machine called Elektro appeared at the New York World Fair. Elektro could say 77 words, sing, and move backwards and forwards.

Sparko, a robot dog built in 1940, could walk, stand on its back legs, and bark.

Just so you know

A robot is a mechanical device which performs a task on its own or under human control. Leonardo da Vinci designed a human-like robot as early as 1495. Czech writer Karel Čapek invented the word "robot" in 1921.

laser device that produces a special kind of pure, powerful light

Robots at work

How would you like a machine to do all your chores? Robots already work in many factories and on assembly lines – but are they safe for home use? In 1984 in Jackson, Michigan, USA a factory robot crushed a worker against an iron bar. It was the first robot-related death in the country. Since then, **laser** light **sensors** have been invented to stop factory robots as soon as anything gets too near them.

Pet robot

Would you want a robot dog in your home? Little iCybie can walk around your house, greet you, wag its tail and give you its paw. It has sensors to make it react to sound, light and touch. It can even respond to commands such as "bad dog", "sit down", "stay", and "guard".

Asimo is a person-sized robot who can walk around corners and up stairs. "Asimo" means Advanced Step in Innovative MObility and is improved year by year.

25

Risking body and mind

Shocking science

When scientists began to find out about electricity in the late 18th century, some thought electric shocks could cure all kinds of illness. They invented devices such as magneto machines that gave small shocks to patients with "nervous disorders". This wouldn't have done any good. It probably made them worse.

Think how rich you would be if you invented something that gave people healthy bodies and happy minds. Many have tried to do this, but failed. However some of them then tried another approach – they lied.

Risky medicine

James Graham was born in Edinburgh, Scotland in 1745 and moved to Philadelphia, USA at the age of 22 years. He called himself "doctor" and tried all kinds of weird cures. He was amazed by Benjamin Franklin's experiments with electricity, and decided: "Electricity **invigorates** the whole body and remedies all physical **defects**." In other words, he claimed electric shocks could be good for you. Wrong!

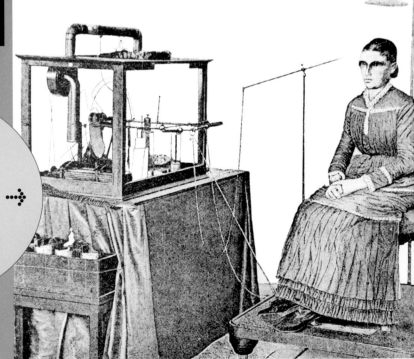

In 1882 machines like this gave electric shocks as "treatment for nerves". No wonder the woman looks so nervous and worried.

Word bank

defect fault or problem
invigorate give life and energy

Sizzling sheets

Graham moved back to London, England in 1775 to sell his false cures. Soon rich and famous people were paying him a lot of money for so-called "health-giving" electric shocks. They didn't know James was a fraud. He set up the Temple of Health in London, equipped with electrical machines such as the "electric bathtub".

Graham's most famous invention was his huge Celestial Bed, where customers paid to sleep. It had perfumed silk sheets and a mattress stuffed with herbs and hair from horses' tails. Using electrical currents and magnets, Graham said it would enable childless couples to have babies. The bed didn't work – but it did make him rich.

Bad advice

James Graham wrote a book for people who wanted to live a long and healthy life. Called *How to Live for Many Weeks or Months or Years Without Eating Anything Whatsoever*, it was hardly based on good science. In fact, Graham starved himself and died of a burst blood vessel in 1794, aged only 49 years.

In this picture from 1780 a "health goddess" uses James Graham's huge Celestial Bed.

Matters of life and death

At one time anyone could say whatever they liked about their medical powers or inventions. False claims about medicines are now against the law.

In the 1870s a housewife from Massachusetts, United States called Lydia Pinkham invented and sold a **tonic**. She claimed it cured cramps and stopped women feeling faint when they wore too-tight corsets. Lydia Pinkham's Vegetable Compound contained only herbs and alcohol, but it sold millions of bottles. By the time Pinkham died in 1883 her invention was earning one million dollars every three years. This carried on until the 1930s, when new laws controlled what adverts could truthfully say about tonics and medicines.

Some medical inventions were more about making money than making people better. Lydia Pinkham (1819–1883) became very rich indeed.

LYDIA E. PINKHAM'S VEGETABLE COMPOUND

IS A POSITIVE CURE
For all those Painful Complaints and Weaknesses
So common among the
Ladies of the World.

Word bank

centrifugal force that pulls outwards from the centre of a fast-spinning object

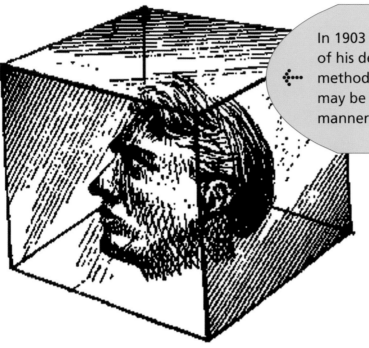

In 1903 Janusz Karkowski said of his dead body preserving method: "The head alone may be preserved in this manner, if preferred."

In 1903 a **patent** was given to Janusz Karkowski in New York, USA, for a new way to preserve a dead body for public viewing. The corpse was encased in a block of glass where it should "keep forever in a perfect and lifelike condition". Not surprisingly, nobody wanted such an outrageous invention.

More false claims

When **radioactive** substances such as radium were discovered from about 1900, at first scientists did not know their dangers. The 1920s saw tonics made of radium mixed in water, to make people strong. One of these tonics was Radithor, made in New Jersey, USA by William Bailey.

Bailey said that Radithor could cure mental illness. A patient called Eben Byers drank 1,400 bottles of it and became seriously ill with radium poisoning. Parts of his mouth and jaw had to be removed, and soon after he died, in 1931. This terrible event was in all the newspapers and led to the end of radium cures.

radioactive giving off particles or rays of energy by the breaking apart of atoms
tonic medicine that makes you feel in good health

Feeling flushed

For centuries, people have worried about their toilet habits. They believed they had to empty their **bowels** regularly. Although this is good advice, people would often panic if they didn't use the toilet every day.

More than 500 years ago, Leonardo da Vinci designed a device to help people open their bowels. It was an **enema** machine, which injected liquid into a person's bottom to make them go to the toilet! Like many of Leonardo's inventions, it was probably not made. His notes were hard to read. He often wrote backwards with one hand while drawing with the other hand.

Ancient idea

Doctors have pushed liquids into patients' bottoms since the time of the ancient Egyptians. Today, enemas are given before some surgery, to wash out the bowels and make treatment **hygienic**. Some modern medicines are also put in the body by enema. Older uses have long since faded, like giving enemas for hiccups!

Rich people in the 1700s paid large sums of money to be given enemas.

Word bank

bowels intestines, body part that holds solid waste
colon main part of the large (lower) bowel

What's for breakfast?

In the early 1900s "**colon** cleansing" treatments were popular, especially in the United States. Dr. John Kellogg (1852–1943) was very keen on the latest enema machines. He flushed out his patients with an enema machine that could pump 70 litres (18 US gallons) of water – about a bathtubful – through the bowel in a few seconds. This was followed by yoghurt. Half was eaten, and the other half was given by yet another enema.

Dr. Kellogg believed that enema treatments kept the body's insides working well and "squeaky clean". He is now best known for another invention – his breakfast cereal. He developed cornflakes as a healthy food that could keep the bowels working properly.

For hundreds of years some Native Americans used hollow bones to push mixtures into their bowels. Around 250 years ago in Europe, enemas were given using large **syringes** invented specially for the task. Louis XIV (1638–1715) of France apparently had over 2,000 enemas during his lifetime.

Dr. John Kellogg held more than 30 **patents** for different food and health products, such as peanut butter, a menthol inhaler and a type of electric blanket.

enema   injection of liquid up a person's bottom, usually to empty the bowels
syringe   plunger-like device to put fluids into the body

Science by mistake

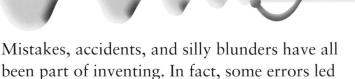

Mistakes, accidents, and silly blunders have all been part of inventing. In fact, some errors led to very useful inventions.

In 1825, Jean-Baptiste Jolly of France spilled **turpentine** from an oil lamp on to his wife's tablecloth. When he tried to rub out the stain, the tablecloth got much cleaner than if he'd used soapy water. He had invented dry-cleaning. As turpentine smells and is **flammable**, modern dry-cleaners now use other liquids.

Snack by accident

In England in about 1762, John Montagu was in a hurry – and invented a popular snack. He was too busy to eat a proper meal and told his cook just to pack meat between slices of bread, to save him time. Montagu was the Earl of Sandwich – and the sandwich was born.

Robert Chesebrough received a **patent** for Vaseline petroleum jelly in 1872. Its name comes from the German word *vasser*, water, and the Greek word *elaion*, oil.

Avoid **Substitutes**

Look for the **TRADE MARK**

Vaseline WHITE PETROLEUM JELLY

In 1859, Robert Chesebrough spotted American oil workers scrubbing waxy material off their oil drills. He tested this and found it could help to ease sores and heal wounds. Eventually he developed this wax into smooth jelly. Chesebrough had invented Vaseline.

Word bank

calorie unit of energy – too many calories in food make you gain weight
flammable able to catch fire easily

They got it wrong

Some people have been totally wrong about new inventions. English scientists laughed at Benjamin Franklin (1706–1790) of the United States, who invented the lightning rod to stop lightning damaging buildings. Yet Franklin turned out to be spot on with his research into lightning and electricity in the 1750s.

English scientist William Thomson said in 1899: "Radio has no future. Heavier-than-air flying machines are impossible. X-rays will prove to be a hoax." How wrong can one person be?

In 1902 German engineers laughed at Ferdinand von Zeppelin. He claimed he'd invented a huge passenger-carrying balloon that could be steered under its own power. Yet Zeppelin airships soon flew many passengers across the Atlantic Ocean.

Count Ferdinand Zeppelin's famous airship *Graf Zeppelin* had passenger cabins, lounges, and dining rooms. In 1929 it flew round the world in 21 days.

Sweet tooth

In 1965 American doctor James Schlatter was developing a new drug to treat ulcers when he spilled some on his fingers. He licked his fingers (not a wise thing to do) and noticed the substance tasted very sweet. Before long it became a fast-selling, low-**calorie** food sweetener, more than 100 times sweeter than sugar, called Nutrasweet.

INTERNATIONALE LUFTSCHIFFAHRT= AUSSTELLUNG FRANKFURT A·M· 1909

turpentine "turps", oil often used as a paint thinner

It wasn't meant to do that!

It's amazing how many inventions have been a surprise. Sometimes an inventor set out to make one thing, discovered a few surprises and ended up inventing something totally different.

Student doctor

Wilson Greatbatch (born in 1919) was an American medical student in the 1950s, working on a device to record the heartbeats of patients with heart disease. One of the machines he used gave little jolts of electricity to keep a patient's heart working, even though it could burn their skin. The machine could control irregular heartbeats, but it was the size of a suitcase.

Lifesaver

Greatbatch then made a mistake that changed heart medicine for ever. He accidentally plugged a wrong piece of equipment into a heartbeat recording machine. It pulsed, stopped, and pulsed again – just like a human heart. A small electrical signal was affecting how it worked. Greatbatch had an idea and quickly got working.

Two years later, in 1958, Greatbatch made a heart **pacemaker** small enough to put inside a patient's chest, to control the heartbeat. He later developed a special small battery to power it.

Delicious surprise

In 1874 Robert Green was selling soda drinks in Philadelphia, USA. One of his drinks was a mixture of cream, syrup, and fizzy water. He ran out of cream one day so he added vanilla ice cream instead, hoping no one would notice. They did and went wild! He'd invented the ice cream soda, which soon sold in millions.

Just so you know

Electricity travels at the speed of light – almost 300,000 kilometres per second (186,000 miles per second). This means it could go around the world seven times in less than one second.

Word bank   pacemaker   electrical device for steadying the heartbeat

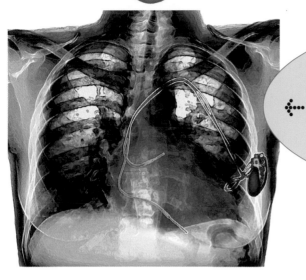

This X-ray shows a heart pacemaker inside a patient. It sends electrical signals along the wires to keep the heart beating regularly.

Greatbatch wrote: "I doubt if anything I ever do will give me the joy I felt that day, when a two-inch electronic device of my own design controlled a living heart."

Walter Diemer (1904–1998) came upon bubble gum by accident, while trying to improve ordinary chewing gum.

The nylon fabric fastener Velcro got its name from two French words, *velour* for velvet, and *crochet* for hook. This name has even been given to a crab that snips off bits of seaweed, to stick on to the hooked hairs all over its body and legs. The weed gives the velcro crab great **camouflage**!

Wearing a Velcro suit, you can stick to a special wall – just like Spiderman!

Getting stuck

It's simple, it sticks, and it keeps millions of people's clothes on! But did you know Velcro was invented by chance, after a country stroll?

In 1948 George de Mestral, a Swiss engineer, arrived home from a walk in the fields. He was covered in tiny plant **burrs** that stuck to his clothes. He loosened them and examined them under his microscope. They had thin strands with hooks on the ends, which clung to the fabric threads of his clothing.

George started experimenting. Eventually he developed two strips of nylon fabric. One had thousands of small hooks and the other had tiny loops. Pressed together, they stuck firmly, yet they could also be separated again. He'd invented Velcro.

Word bank

burr rough or prickly case of a fruit or seed
camouflage hiding or disguising something by changing how it looks

Singing science

Spencer Silver was an American scientist who tried to develop a new strong glue in the 1970s. His efforts weren't very good – the result was very weak glue. It stuck things but they could easily be pulled apart again. No one knew what to do with the stuff.

Arthur Fry worked with Silver. He sang in a choir and used markers to keep his place in a songbook. The markers kept falling out so he tried coating them with Silver's glue. The markers stayed in place, yet lifted off without damaging the pages. Post-It Notes had arrived!

Sticky reminders

Post-It Notes began to sell across the United States in 1980. Today they come in all shapes, colours, and sizes, stuck everywhere to jog our memories. By the year 2000 this "failed glue" was said to earn its company around one billion dollars a year.

Arthur Fry had the idea of using a partly-sticky glue on paper to make "peelable" Post-It Notes.

Super-stuck

Have you ever wondered at the secrets of the strongest glues you can buy? Super-glue was invented by accident in the 1940s by Harry Coover in the United States. While working in a lab during World War II, he found that some of the chemicals he was mixing became too sticky to handle. Moisture made the chemicals bond together. He had to throw them away and start again.

Years later Coover remembered his mixture, and he tried making the extra strong glue again. He found it could stick almost anything. A few drops can now fix a broken vase faster than you can say "Oops!".

Old glue, new glue

For centuries glues were made from the boiled bones of animals or the sticky **resins** of plants. **Synthetic** glues such as super-glue are chemicals made from oil, called petrochemicals. When super-glue is exposed to moisture in the air, its tiny particles or **molecules** join together to form a strong, instant bond.

Modern glues are said to stick almost anything, even two cars on to a billboard sign. ⋯⫶

The tension mounts.

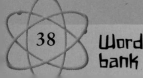
molecule smallest particle of a substance which has all the features or characteristics of that substance

A microscope shows the threads in mussel glue that fix the shell to a rock. That's real mussel power!

Nature's super-glue

In 2004 scientists unlocked some of the secrets of nature's own super-glue. They may soon be able to make even stronger glues by copying the tricks of a sea creature.

Marine biologists discovered how sea mussels stick to rocks in the roughest sea. It seems a key ingredient is iron in the glue that coats mussel shells. Knowing how such glue is formed could lead scientists to invent new coatings and glues for the future. Surgeons are already working on using glues instead of stitches to repair a patient's wounds.

Super-glue catches criminals

In 1982 Japanese scientists made an accidental discovery when they fixed a crack in a fish tank with super-glue. Their fingerprints on the glass stood out clearly. The fumes from the super-glue had reacted with natural skin oils from the scientists' fingers. Now super-glue helps police when they search for fingerprints.

resins substances from the gum or sap of some trees
synthetic not natural but made by people

Science in the kitchen

A lot of the "fast food" we eat today is the result of recipes carefully developed over years by chefs, scientists or food companies. However sometimes accidents can lead to fantastic and tasty inventions.

In 1853, a Native American called George Crum worked as a chef in New York. One dinner guest complained that Crum's french fries (chipped potatoes) were far too thick. Crum decided to show the customer that thinner chips would be much too crunchy. He cut the potatoes into outrageously thin slices. He thought that would teach the customer a lesson. But Crum's plan backfired…

Unexpected magic

Ruth Wakefield was baking chocolate biscuits in the 1930s in Massachusetts, USA. She put chunks of a chocolate bar into the batter, expecting them to melt. Instead, she made butter cookies studded with gooey chocolate lumps. Her mistake turned into one of the favourite treats of all time – chocolate chip cookies.

Factories around the world churn out billions of potato crisps every year – including new healthier, lower-fat versions.

Crunching round the world

When George Crum presented the grumpy customer with curled-up, brown, paper-thin potatoes, there was a gasp of excitement. The crunchy chips were great and all the diners wanted Crum's crisp potato slices.

Factories soon began making packets of Crum's invention by the thousands. With the invention of the mechanical potato peeler in the 1920s, potato crisps were no longer made by hand, and millions more could be produced.

The huge industry that George Crum triggered in 1853 keeps growing. Called potato chips in the United States and crisps in the United Kingdom, they are favourite snacks almost everywhere. Sales in the United States are more than US$6 billion a year. Not so much "healthy eating" as "wealthy eating"!

This is one of the first Coca-Cola adverts from 1900. The Coca-Cola company now sells about one billion drinks around the world every day.

41

Thousands of weird inventions never earned their creators any money at all. Even if they were actually produced, they just didn't catch on. This is hardly surprising when you see how outrageous they could be.

The rowing bicycle

"I, Louis Burbank, a citizen of the United States, and a resident of Worcester, Mass., have invented useful improvements in bicycles. The object of the invention is to provide exercise like that of rowing, which develops the muscles of the arms and body as well as those of the legs." Don't try this 1900 idea in your local street!

Get me out of here!

For centuries people worried about being buried before they were actually dead. Inventor William White made an alarm system in 1891 for anyone waking up in a coffin deep under the ground. But fitting coffins with his alarm-pull mechanism didn't catch on.

Would you risk Louis Burbank's row-cycle? It could be tricky in city traffic!

Sunk without trace

Have you ever needed to walk on water? If so, Martin Jelaian's invention of 1918 could be for you. He developed a device for walking on water in Rhode Island, USA. It used a gas-filled balloon strapped to a person's body, and boards on the feet with air-bags to help them float. A hand support was meant to stop the walker falling while "sliding upon the surface of the water in a perfectly safe and successful manner." Obviously Jelaian didn't make his fortune. People preferred another useful invention for water travel – the boat!

A scary way to wake up

US Patent No. 256,265, issued in 1882, was: A Device for Waking Persons from Sleep. "In my invention I hang a frame directly over the head of the sleeper. At the proper time the frame falls into the sleeper's face, giving a light blow to awaken the sleeper, but not heavy enough to cause pain." An alarm clock is much safer.

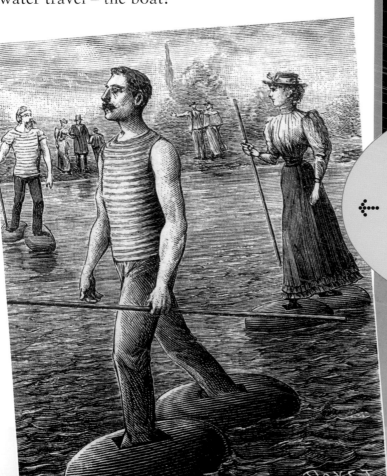

These sea-boots of 1895 did not catch on, probably because anyone wearing them could fall over and never get up again!

Can you believe it?

Some inventions given **patents** over the last 150 years:
- A ladder for spiders to climb out of the bath.
- A two-handed glove for people who wish to hold hands and keep in touch in cold weather.
- Spectacles for chickens to stop them pecking each other's eyes.

In the 1970s in Britain, Clive Sinclair was a successful inventor of calculators and computers. In 1985 he tried a more outrageous idea. One of his wacky inventions was a way to get around town by beating the traffic – if you dared.

The Sinclair C5 was a one-person, battery-operated "car". It didn't catch on. The machine could only travel at 24 kilometres per hour (15 miles per hour) because at the time, electric vehicles that went faster needed a special licence. The main problem was that it couldn't go far before the battery ran down – maybe only 10 kilometres (6.2 miles) in cold weather. In the rain, the driver got soaked.

Clive Sinclair tries out his C5 electric tricycle in London, England. About 12,000 were made. The electric motor came from a washing machine!

A bright idea

In 2005 an American inventor began selling his Brightfeet slippers. Doug Vick got the idea after getting up in the night and bumping his feet on a bedpost. The next day his sore feet, and the idea that millions of people do the same, encouraged him to invent slippers with torches in the toes. If it's dark, beams of light come on when feet slide into the slippers. When they are taken off, a timer keeps the light on long enough for the person to get back into bed. Night trips to the bathroom or fridge have never been safer!

Travel of the future?

How would you like to travel around town on a Segway Human Transporter? Invented by American Dean Kamen in 2001, the Segway is the world's first two-wheeled, self-balancing transport machine. Computers and motors in the base keep it upright. Users lean forward to go ahead or lean back for reverse.

The Segway, here being tested by Boston police in the United States, reaches speeds of 20 kilometres per hour (12.5 miles per hour).

In the news

Inventions of all kinds are often in the news. Some of them might change the world while others will fizzle away without trace. Inventors are always at work and some of today's ideas can be just as outrageous as those from long ago.

Diet robot is barking!

How about a robot dog that helps its owner to lose weight? The Japanese-American dog can monitor its owner's diet and exercise, and then give a health report. The dog is linked to bathroom weighing scales. If the owner loses weight the dog dances, flashes lights, and plays music as a reward. It begs a question – who's training who?

Robot fish

In 2005, the world's first self-controlled fish robot went on show at the London Aquarium, England. It can swim as fast as tuna and navigate as well as an eel, using **sensor** controls. Inventor Professor Huosheng Hu said that the fishy robots have many uses, such as detecting leaks in oil pipelines and checking under ships and boats.

Professor Hu's robo-fish swims like the real thing and controls itself so it does not bump into objects.

Word bank

remote   far away from towns and cities

Wind-up technology

A great invention that has become a huge success in **remote** areas of the world was developed in the 1990s. British engineer Trevor Baylis devised a wind-up radio that needs no new batteries. Turning a clockwork handle recharges the batteries inside. At last people anywhere can listen to the radio.

In 2005 a clockwork laptop computer was invented in Massachusetts, USA. It is also very inexpensive. It's hoped that millions of children in poorer countries around the world will be able to use these computers where there is no reliable electricity supply.

New outrageous chemistry

The Nissan Motor Company has created a car paint that repairs scratches by itself. Within a week, a small scratch will "heal". Nissan said the speed of this amazing self-repair depends on the temperature and the size of the scratch. Scratch Guard Coat protects for three years and was first used on production cars in 2006.

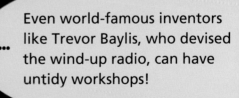

Even world-famous inventors like Trevor Baylis, who devised the wind-up radio, can have untidy workshops!

47

Weird science in the 21st century

What will the outrageous inventions of tomorrow be like? Some scientists believe that important developments of the future will be very tiny robots called **nanorobots**. They are smaller than the head of a pin. These microscopic robots could have many uses. They might be put into the body to fight germs and diseases. They could carry medicine to the exact site where it is needed. They could even repair parts of the brain from the inside. How amazing is that?

More inventors wanted

There are still big problems for inventors to solve in the future. How can we make enough clean energy for the world, instead of burning **fossil fuels** in cars, homes, factories, and power stations? The scientists who invent ways to create plenty of cheap, clean energy could be the rich heroes of tomorrow.

This computer image shows how a nanorobot could inject one of the body's microscopic cells with medicine.

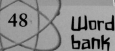

Word bank fossil fuels fuels such as coal, oil, or natural gas that formed inside Earth over a long time from plant or animal remains

Inventing never stops

Life in the 21st century should be easier than ever before, thanks to the millions of inventions we have today. What would you list as your top ten inventions of all time? Would ten be enough? (See page 50 for some suggestions.)

American writer Ralph Waldo Emerson (1803–1882) once said: "Build a better mousetrap, and the world will beat a path to your door." Since then, about 4,500 United States **patents** have been issued for mousetrap designs. This makes the mousetrap the most invented machine in American history. Yet still people come up with more designs. Maybe this book has inspired you to invent yet another one!

(See page 50 for some suggestions.)

Tomorrow's world?

In the 21st century, wars may be fought by robots rather than by human soldiers. The United States army may have human-like robots in use by 2025. Already some types of robots play a part on the battlefield. Many weapons are remote-controlled. Robots may even become the inventors of tomorrow!

Could a future battle be fought between robot soldiers? Or should inventors turn their skills to ways of avoiding war?

nanorobot tiny automatic machine, far too small to see

Inventions timeline

These amazing inventions were all thought to be outrageous in their day. What do you think about them now?

1643   In Italy, Evangelista Torricelli builds a barometer for measuring air pressure, which we now use to forecast the weather

1816   Karl von Sauerbronn in Germany devises an early form of bicycle

1827   Charles Wheatstone in Britain develops an early type of microphone to turn sound waves in air into electrical signals

1829   William Burt receives a United States **patent** on the first mechanical writing machine – the typewriter

1841   Antoine Joseph Sax in France works on the musical instrument that bears his name, the saxophone

1862   War becomes more deadly with the machine gun, invented by Richard Jordan Gatling of the United States

1867   Swedish chemist Alfred Nobel invents the powerful explosive dynamite

1873   Joseph Glidden of the United States keeps people and animals in (or out) with barbed wire

1890   A new form of execution, the electric chair, is developed in the United States by Harold Brown and Arthur Kennelly

1893   American master inventor Thomas Edison works on an early form of motion pictures, later altered into its modern form by the Lumière Brothers in France

1899	At last people could hold together sheets of paper, courtesy of Norwegian Johann Waaler's paper clip
1902	Life becomes cooler with the air conditioner, invented by Willis Carrier in the United States
1914	Ernest Swinton of Britain works on the military fighting machine we call the tank
1932	Carlton Magee of the United States is to blame for that annoying city street gadget, the parking meter
1936	Where would holidaymakers be without suntan lotion, thanks to Eugene Schueller of France
1947	Percy Spencer of the United States builds the first practical microwave oven – ping!
1979	Personal music began with the Sony Walkman, from Akio Morita of Japan
1995	The world's biggest electronics, television, computer and entertainments companies work together and invent the DVD (digital versatile disc) to replace videotape
2004	A new generation of mobile phones begin to take and send pictures and videos, and even receive live television broadcasts
2004	*Popular Science* magazine chooses, as its best invention for leisure and recreation, the Adidas 1 "intelligent trainers". A built-in microchip decides whether the wearer needs soft or firm support.
2005	Two new versions of the DVD are announced, but each will not work in the player designed for the other. So much for working together.

Find out more

Using the Internet

Explore the Internet to find out more about the history of inventions or to see pictures of famous inventors and their inventions.

You can use a search engine such as **www.yahooligans.com**

Or ask a question at **www.ask.com**

Type in key words such as
• Leonardo da Vinci
• ornithopter
• Thomas Alva Edison
• robots
• gadgets and inventions

There are fun lists and "signposts" for many different sites on inventors and inventions at **www.kidskonnect.com/Invent/InventionsHome.html**

You can find information about inventions over the last 10,000 years that have changed the way we live at **www.cbc.ca/kids/general/the-lab/history-of-invention/default.html**

Books

You can find out more about strange science and outrageous inventions by looking at other books.

Binney, Ruth (editor). *The Origins of Everyday Things* (Reader's Digest, 1999)

Bridgman, Roger. *Eyewitness Guides: Technology* (Dorling Kindersley, 1998)

Ganeri, Anita. *Inside and Out Guides: Great Inventions* (Heinemann, 2006)

Twist, Clint. *Inside and Out Guides: Mighty Machines* (Heinemann, 2006)

Internet search tips

There are billions of pages on the Internet so it can be difficult to find exactly what you are looking for.

These search tips will help you find websites more quickly:

- Know exactly what you want to find out about first.
- Use two to six keywords in a search, putting the most important words first.
- Be precise. Only use names of people, places, or things.

Computer control by thinking

A computer controlled just by the power of thought has been on display in Germany. It could help paralysed people to use computers and similar devices like computer games consoles. The Berlin Brain-Computer Interface (BBCI) makes it possible to type messages on to a computer screen by mentally controlling the movement of a cursor. The user wears a cap that measures electrical activity inside the brain and then sends signals to the computer. What will inventors think of next?

Glossary

bowels intestines, body part that holds solid waste

burr rough or prickly case of a fruit or seed

calorie unit of energy – too many calories in food make you gain weight

camouflage hiding or disguising something by changing how it looks

centrifugal force that pulls outwards from the centre of a fast-spinning object

cistern tank for storing water

colon main part of the large (lower) bowel

defect fault or problem

enema injection of liquid up a person's bottom, usually to empty the bowels

fad short-lived fashion or interest

flammable able to catch fire easily

fossil fuels fuels such as coal, oil, or natural gas that formed inside Earth over a long time from plant or animal remains

genius very gifted person with great abilities

hygiene cleanliness, keeping germ-free to stay healthy

inspiration having a great thought or idea

internal combustion when power comes from fuel burning in an enclosed space

invigorate give life and energy

jaywalker someone on a road who pays little attention to traffic

laser device that produces a special kind of pure, powerful light

molecule smallest particle of a substance which has all the features or characteristics of that substance

nanorobot tiny automatic machine, far too small to see

ornithopter flying machine with wings that flap like a bird's

pacemaker electrical device for steadying the heartbeat

patent special document giving only the inventor the right to make and sell the invention

pedestrian walking person

perspiration sweat

pneumatic worked by air, such as pumping air under pressure

pollution chemicals, particles
or rubbish that spoil or
damage nature

radioactive giving off particles or
rays of energy by the breaking
apart of atoms

reflector object which bounces
back or reflects light

remote far away from towns
and cities

resin substance from the gum or
sap of some trees

sensor device that detects what
is nearby

solo done by or for one person

synthetic not natural but made
by people

syringe plunger-like device to put
fluids into the body

telegraph method of sending
messages along wires as code
signals, such as Morse Code

tonic medicine that makes you feel
in good health

turpentine "turps", oil often used
as a paint thinner

vulcanize treat rubber with
chemicals and heat to give
it strength

Index

Titles in the *Weird History of Science* series include:

Hardback 978-1-4062-0556-5

Hardback 978-1-4062-0558-9

Hardback 978-1-4062-0557-2

Hardback 978-1-4062-0559-6

Find out about the other titles in this series on our website www.raintreepublishers.co.uk